Management

GUY BROWNING

Grass Roots Management

How to grow initiative and responsibility

in all your people

Prentice
Hall

BUSINESS

An imprint of **Pearson Education**

London • New York • Toronto • Sydney • Tokyo • Singapore • Hong Kong • Cape Town
New Delhi • Madrid • Paris • Amsterdam • Munich • Milan • Stockholm

PEARSON EDUCATION LIMITED

Head Office:
Edinburgh Gate
Harlow CM20 2JE
Tel: +44 (0)1279 623623
Fax: +44 (0)1279 431059

London Office:
128 Long Acre
London WC2E 9AN
Tel: +44 (0)20 7447 2000
Fax: +44 (0)20 7447 2170
Websites: www.business-minds.com
          www.yourmomentum.com

First published in Great Britain in 2003

© Guy Browning 2003

The right of Guy Browning to be identified as Author
of this Work has been asserted by him in accordance
with the Copyright, Designs and Patents Act 1988.

© Colin Shelbourn (www.shelbourn.com) for the illustrations

ISBN 0273 66299 6

British Library Cataloguing in Publication Data
A CIP catalogue record for this book can be obtained from the British Library

10 9 8 7 6 5 4 3 2

Designed by Claire Brodmann Book Designs, Lichfield, Staffs
Typeset by Northern Phototypesetting Co. Ltd, Bolton
Printed and bound in Great Britain by Bookcraft, Midsomer Norton

The Publishers' policy is to use paper manufactured from sustainable forests.

Guy Browning is a columnist for
the *Guardian*, *Management Today* and *People Management*.

This book is dedicated with love
to Ralph and Amanda
who can manage just about anything

A big thank you ...

... to Esther Browning, Fiona McAnena, Ed McCabe, Martin Glenn, Chris Harrison, David Rea, Rachael Stock and Richard Stagg. Without them this book would have been considerably thicker.

Contents

Chapter One

The Gardens

It was a lovely, sunny Monday morning and John arrived at The Gardens early. He wanted to make a good impression as it was his first day in his new job. At the front entrance of the gardens he approached the security man at the gate and said: 'It's my first day.'

'Whoopee,' the security man replied without bothering to look up.

'Where do I go?'

'I suppose you'd better go up to the Big House,' he said, waving John up the long, winding road behind the gate.

John passed through the gate and began walking up the long road to the Big House. The gardens were very big and he couldn't see the Big House. Fortunately, there was a large map a few yards up the road. From the map he could see that The Gardens were separated into North, South, East and West gardens with the Big House set in the middle. He also noticed that the paint was peeling from the map. The place where it should have said 'You are here' was worn away by continual use. No surprise, perhaps, because The Gardens attracted tourists and garden lovers from far and wide.

John started walking up the road, looking around him at the gardens as he went. There were many lovely beds of flowers and shrubs and a host of large and small trees. In between there were stretches of lawn, both formal and informal.

John loved gardens and gardening. To his mind there was nothing more satisfying than planning a garden, planting it carefully, looking after it and watching it grow. He took a deep breath, full of the scent of honeysuckle, and decided that this was going to be the job of a lifetime.

As he breathed in deeply, his foot hit a tin can. John instinctively picked up the can and looked around for a bin to put it in. There wasn't one. Two hundred yards farther up the path he found one, full to overflowing and surrounded by angry wasps. Not good, he thought.

John then began to notice many little things about the garden that were not as good as they seemed at first sight. The lawns weren't cut as close as they should be. On closer inspection, many of the borders were full of weeds. Even some of the big trees were beginning to lose their shape for want of careful surgery.

John loved gardens and gardening. To his mind there was nothing more satisfying than planning a garden, planting it carefully, looking after it and watching it grow.

Rounding a bend in the road between two big rhododendron bushes, John came across what looked like a tropical garden. There were many strange species in it, all of which looked in a bad way. Many were dead, others were clearly dying. John was increasingly confused and disappointed. This was not what he had expected to find in The Gardens which, after all, had such a great reputation.

But then John rounded another corner and saw the Big House, sitting majestically in the morning sun surrounded by beautifully manicured lawns. This was more like it. The house hadn't yet opened so John sat down on a bench and enjoyed the view.

I tell them every year we want to be the best garden in the world. I tell them that it's down to them. I tell them they're empowered. But nothing happens.

Presently a man came along and sat down on the bench next to John. He was about fifty and looked as though he owned the place.

'Lovely morning,' said John.

'Yes, I suppose it is,' said the man, looking round as if noticing the gardens for the first time.

'Lovely gardens,' said John.

'Do you think so?' The man gave him a searching stare.

'Well . . .' said John. He didn't know who the man was and didn't want to risk offending him.

'They're my gardens. I've just done my inspection and they're not really up to scratch,' the man said and then continued before John could think of a reply. 'It's the gardeners. I can't do the whole thing myself. I tell them every year we want to be the best garden in the world. I tell them that it's down to them. I tell them they're empowered. But nothing happens. Nothing changes.' The man shook his head with frustration.

'I see,' John said neutrally.

'Look at this broken slat.' The man pointed to the back of the bench on which they were sitting. 'If I hadn't noticed it and if I don't now go and shout at a few people, it won't get mended. And then pretty soon we'd have lots of benches without slats, our visitors will be falling through them and no-one would give a monkey's except me.'

'I see,' said John. It did seem to be a problem, but John wasn't quite sure what to do about it or what to say to this man who was clearly the boss.

'See this lawn?' the man continued.

'Yes.' How was the man going to complain about the lawn, John thought. It looked immaculate.

'This lawn is immaculate. Do you know why that is?'

'No,' said John, sensing he was about to find out.

'Because it's the one I can see from my office,' the man said, pointing to a window high up in the house.

'Right,' said John, nodding his head in sympathy.

'This is the sixth year I've told them they're empowered,' the man said sadly. 'Just one morning I'd like to come in and find something good had been done without me specifically order-ing it.' He walked off shaking his head.

The man disappeared into the Big House and John decided to get moving. He didn't want the man staring out of his window at him especially if he was the Big Boss, which John was beginning to suspect he was. Instead, John walked round to the other side of the house, noticing immediately that the North lawns were not quite as well kept as those on the South. He also saw what looked like a folly in the trees on the other side of the lawns, so he made his way towards it.

As he approached the folly he saw it was actually some kind of building that was only half-built and was half covered with ugly, fast-growing conifers. At one end of the building a gar-dener sat on a large log reading a paper and drinking a cup of coffee from a flask. He saw John and waved him over.

'Morning,' said John.

'Lovely morning,' said the gardener.

'It's my first day,' said John.

'Good for you,' said the gardener. 'No point in rushing into it. Have a coffee.'

The gardener poured John a coffee. 'I saw you having a chat with the Big Boss.'

'Yes. He wasn't very happy. He seemed to think that no-one

bothered to do anything in the garden without him telling them.'

'That sounds pretty typical. He's been telling us what to do for six years now.'

'So why haven't you done it?' asked John politely.

'It's your first day isn't it?'

'Yes.'

'You'll learn.'

❧ Talk to any manager and they will tell you, very quietly, of a secret wish. One morning they would like to come into their office and find, sitting in their in-tray, a solution rather than a problem.

❧ Talk to any manager and they will tell you that their door is always open. One day they would really like someone to walk through it and talk to them.

❧ The trouble is that everybody's heard of empowerment. But no-one's ever seen it.

❧ And if you talk to managers and business leaders for some time, they will tell you that they are confused.

❧ They know their teams are decent, hardworking people and they themselves also try to be decent, hardworking managers. They also know that everyone wants a growing, successful company in which everyone can be proud.

❧ Yet it still seems monumentally difficult to improve things, to change things and to make things happen.

❧ Managers often complain that all they do is 'wheelbarrow management' – that is, if they're not taking the strain and pushing like hell, nothing moves.

❧ The higher up managers are, the more they complain about this.

❧ But then if you talk to the people who work on the front line, they'll tell you a different story.

Chapter Two

The Gardeners

After finishing their coffee, John and the other gardener, whose name was Steve, walked back through the garden. The early morning mist was still clinging to the lawns and John thought once more how lucky he was to be paid to work in a garden.

'We've got our team briefing this morning,' said Steve.

'What happens there?' asked John.

'We're told what needs doing in the garden and who's going to do it.'

They passed a low hedge that was damaged in several places where visitors had been forcing their way through, probably as a short cut.

As they talked, they passed a low hedge that was damaged in several places where visitors had been forcing their way through, probably as a short cut.

It took ten minutes to walk to the team briefing in the South Garden. John realized just how big The Gardens were and it came as no surprise to him that there were a large number of gardeners at the briefing, all gathered in an old wooden building that looked like a large shed. On the walls of the shed were pinned a number of attractive posters. While he was waiting for the meeting to start, John walked round the room reading them. There were posters on teamwork, customers, the environment, responsibility, coaching and empowerment. Each had a beautiful picture and some lovely poetic words underneath. 'This must be a great place to work,' John thought to himself.

The Senior Gardener introduced himself as Kevin and welcomed John to the South Gardens. He then started the team briefing to the assembled gardeners.

'This month, the target we have been given is three thousand visitors.'

There was a general sigh around the room accompanied by one or two hollow laughs.

Kevin ignored them and continued. 'And just to remind you, the priorities for this month are weeding and path maintenance.'

'We should have done the weeding last month after that downpour,' a woman from the back said.

Kevin nodded in agreement. 'Well, Catherine, we would have done if it wasn't for the push on composting.'

Catherine made to say something else, but decided against it, shrugged her shoulders and kept quiet.

'I've heard the West Gardens are bedding out some begonias,' an old gardener said from beside John. 'We could do with some of those by the lower lawn.'

'I don't think we've got any of those planned,' Kevin replied, consulting his clipboard. 'You could always ask if they've got any spares,' he added rather despairingly.

There was a silence around the room. John seized his moment and said: 'I passed a box hedge on the way here that needs some attention.'

'Well spotted, John.' Kevin smiled. 'We've all noticed that one, but it doesn't seem to have got in the plan yet,' he said, tapping his clipboard. 'Stick with Steve. He'll show you what to do.'

After the meeting Steve and John walked back towards the Big House, passing the early visitors. Shortly, they arrived at a large bed full of weeds. Two ladies were looking at the bed and pointing to one of the bushy, golden-yellow shrubs and arguing about its name. John was about to go and tell them it was a Jocasta. He had one in his garden at home and it was his special favourite.

Just then Steve grabbed his arm. 'No,' he said.

John looked at him with surprise. 'Why not?'

'Because we're not allowed to talk to visitors. They've paid their money and we mustn't interfere.'

'But I was only trying to help.'

'Trying and helping aren't in the plan yet,' Steve said, tapping an imaginary clipboard with a slightly embarrassed smile.

After two hours weeding, the bed was looking in much better shape. They stopped for a break and John asked a question he'd been wondering about all morning. 'Why do they give us targets for visitor numbers?'

'Well, the Big House sets the targets. They've probably been told to by the bankers.'

'Then why do they tell us what to do in the garden.'

'Because they can plan on a large scale to make sure everything gets done. They can do things more efficiently,' Steve said without much conviction.

'It didn't look like it this morning.'

John drank the rest of his coffee in silence. He was beginning to feel a little bit disappointed. He had the job he always wanted in the famous Gardens but things weren't quite right and he couldn't put his finger on exactly what.

> He had the job he always wanted in the famous Gardens but things weren't quite right and he couldn't put his finger on exactly what.

'It didn't seem like a terribly happy meeting this morning,' he said tentatively.

'Oh, that was a pretty good meeting. You should see them when we get upset about something. Don't get me wrong, they're a really good bunch. If you ever need a hand, they'd do anything for you. And between us, there's not a lot we don't know about gardening.'

'Well surely you should be having more of a say in what to do in the garden.'

'It's a big garden. It's a big business. It's out of our hands,' Steve replied with a shrug.

'It must be very frustrating sometimes.'

'It can be,' Steve said carefully, 'And occasionally we do tend to lose some very good people. But it's still a great job.'

John thought about this long and hard. Finally he said. 'It just doesn't seem to be the natural way of doing things.' And for a gardener, that was a very serious criticism indeed.

'Don't worry about things out of your control,' said Steve. 'We've got the big party tomorrow, that'll cheer you up.'

'Big party?'

'Yes, it happens like clockwork every year. It's when we're all empowered and given a free bar.'

'A free bar,' John repeated. 'I like the sound of that.'

Staff often believe they are the helpless victims of change in the company. They think they aren't listened to and they don't think initiative is any part of their job.

ॐ This isn't surprising. Many companies have taken a lot of costs out of their business. The biggest cost is always people, so they've reduced the number of people to the absolute minimum. What's left are some very efficient, very hard-working, slightly scared people.

ॐ Given enough time and encouragement, these people would tell you what works about the business and what doesn't work.

ॐ But normally they won't tell you. Because they are no longer inspired by their job, they no longer feel engaged in their job and they don't feel they have the power to change things for the better.

ॐ They've survived by being efficient and cutting costs. They know that ideas generally look like costs and that any-thing that looks like a cost has a very short life span. Even worse, they believe having ideas will only increase their own workload.

ॐ The relationship between staff and management has now become: 'Tell me what you want and I'll do it.' Which doesn't make either party happy.

ॐ Managers increasingly recognize this problem, which is the good news. The bad news is they then make a big mistake.

ॐ They call in the consultants.

Chapter Three

The Expert Gardeners

Planting the seeds of growth

When John arrived for work the following day he found that a large marquee had been erected on the South lawn of the Big House. Technicians in black shirts were buzzing around the marquee and he could hear the sound of the public address system being tested.

'One two. One two. Testing. One two.' It all seemed very exciting.

It seemed to be a montage of great sporting moments mixed with close-ups of trowels, spades and forks being thrust into the ground.

One hour later, all the gardeners from the South Garden filed into the big marquee. Inside were all the gardeners from the West, East and North gardens, many of whom he'd never seen before. They took their places in the rows of chairs and looked at the big stage. On the stage was a big screen that said, 'Planting The Seeds for Growth'.

There was a good atmosphere in the marquee as everyone chattered away and enjoyed their day off. Suddenly, there was a blast of music and a video on the screen. It seemed to be a montage of great sporting moments mixed with close-ups of trowels, spades and forks being thrust into the ground.

When it finished, the Big Boss arrived on the stage. He gave a speech about the garden and how growth was vital. He then showed some complex-looking figures on some charts behind him. He finished by telling everyone that the 'seeds for growth' were in their hands and it was up to them to plant them. Everyone clapped loudly. The Big Boss knew how to make a good speech, even if much of it didn't mean anything to John and the gardeners.

There followed speeches by the Head of Planning, the Head of Buying and the Head of Sales. Finally, the Head of Personnel came on and talked to the gardeners about culture change, empowerment and coaching skills. This was all a complete mystery to John but she seemed nice enough and everyone listened politely.

Finally, the Big Boss popped up again and told everyone that 'Planting the seeds of growth' wasn't just a one-off, it was to become a way of life in the gardens. There was more applause, principally because the free bar was now very close at hand.

The gardeners made for the free bar and it wasn't long before the party was in full swing and virtually everything that had been said on the stage was forgotten.

After a while John decided to go out for some fresh air. He found Catherine, one of the South gardeners, sitting on a bench and joined her.

'Well John, what did you make of your first conference?' she asked as he sat down next to her.

'It was a great video but I'm not sure what most of the others were talking about.'

'I shouldn't worry. It's what they do in the Big House. It's not really relevant to us.'

'Well, what happens now with "Planting the seeds of growth."?'

'If past conferences are anything to go by, then in tomorrow's meeting we'll have a special team briefing, we'll be given something colourful with "seeds of growth" on it somewhere and we'll be asked for our ideas to improve the garden.'

John laughed. Catherine seemed very cynical for someone so young. After a while they went back into the marquee and enjoyed the rest of the evening.

The following morning, in the team meeting, John found a bag with his name on. Inside there was a nicely designed file with 'Planting the seeds of growth' written on it containing summaries of all the previous day's speeches. John reached further into the bag and pulled out a little plastic trowel on the back of which was written, 'Planting the seeds of growth'.

Kevin turned up and the team meeting began. He laid what seemed to be a board game on the table. The game was called

'Planting the seeds of growth'. It was a beautifully designed map of the garden. Everyone was given sticky notes and had to put their ideas for improving the garden on the board.

'So, anybody got any bright ideas?' Kevin asked, not very hopefully.

Nobody said anything. Over the years everybody had had plenty of ideas for improving the garden but these had long been forgotten.

'Come on everybody,' Kevin pleaded. 'Give me something I can give the Big House.'

The gardeners sighed and wrote down ideas they'd had a thousand times before but had long since given up hope of ever seeing come to life. They placed their notes on the board and John noticed that all the notes were put down in the South garden. John added one about gardeners working together across the four gardens, which he placed for effect in the North Garden. No-one seemed to notice. Then the team meeting was over and everyone went back to work, leaving their bags and plastic trowels behind them.

John walked with his friend Steve up to the beds they were working on that day. They passed some outside contractors with diggers ripping up a corner of one of the lawns.

'What's going on there?' John asked, slightly shocked at the sight of the lawn disappearing.

'It's the new Chinese Garden. The expert gardeners have said that all things Chinese are very fashionable in gardens at the moment. Apparently the visitors will come flocking in.'

'Why didn't they ask us about it?'

'We're not the experts. We're not paid enough to be experts.'

'We still know about gardening.'

> *The garden experts work on all the big gardens and they know what's going on in the big, wide world.*

'Yes, but the garden experts work on all the big gardens and they know what's going on in the big, wide world.'

'But are they actually gardeners? Do they get their hands dirty?'

'No, they're more conceptual gardeners. They think about gardening.'

John was shocked into silence. If half the money they were obviously spending on the new Chinese Garden went to making some much-needed improvements around the garden as a whole, it would make a huge difference. Especially to the gardeners who worked in it.

A little further down the road they passed the old tropical garden with the dead and dying plants. John looked at the remains of the tropical garden. 'Don't tell me. This was one of the expert gardeners' ideas.'

'Yep. Exactly three years ago. Part of "Digging the Future" if I remember correctly. I've still got the plastic wheelbarrow at home somewhere.'

  There are two types of consultants. The first are the good consultants, which are companies that have specialist skills you don't have in your organization.

  Then there are the bad consultants who have skills that you already have in your organization but who claim to do things better than you. Employing the first kind of consultant is good for your business. Employing the second is almost always bad.

  Bad consultants feed on the ignorance, laziness and insecurity of managers. The worst consultants only know two things: they know how to look clever and they know how to make the people who employ them look clever.

  Such consultants claim to add value. This generally means that their basic product isn't up to much and to make money they want to do your thinking for you. These consultants give the impression that they have better people, better clothes, better education, better cars, better offices and better Danish pastries with their better coffee.

❧ You can choose to be impressed by this or you can ask yourself three simple questions: Why can't we do that thinking for ourselves? Do we have that kind of expertise in the company already? If we haven't, can we grow it ourselves?

❧ What all consultants do know is how to play the internal politics of an organization. They know how decisions are made. They know how budgets are allocated. Most of all, they know how senior managers behave.

❧ Bad consultants wouldn't exist if it weren't for senior managers willing to pay for them. So what's wrong with senior managers?

Chapter Four

The Garden Director

That morning John arrived early for work. It was something he often did because he liked getting up early and he liked being able to enjoy the gardens before the visitors and other gardeners started arriving.

He sat down on a bench on the South lawns. It had been two months since he had joined The Gardens. Since then, many aspects of the garden and the way it was managed had disappointed him. On mornings like this he often thought how much better it could be with only a little effort and a few changes.

As he was thinking these thoughts he saw the Big Boss coming towards him. John's immediate thought was to get up and go. John had learned in the last two months that it was generally not a profitable or life-enhancing experience to talk to the garden managers.

'Good morning,' the Big Boss said, before John could move a muscle.

'Morning,' John replied, mentally checking if he'd made any obvious mistakes in the garden recently.

'Haven't we met before?' the Big Boss asked as he sat down next to John.

'We have. It was my first day.'

'Oh yes, I remember. How's it going?'

John thought for a second. Should he tell the man what he really thought? It was such a nice morning, why spoil it? Then from nowhere, John asked a completely different question.

'You're the Garden Director, aren't you.'

'I am.' The director looked at John sharply, as if expecting bad news.

'So you're in charge of The Gardens?'

'Yes, that's right.' The director now looked very much on his guard.

'Well,' John paused, 'what exactly do you do all day?'

There was a silence during which John considered various career options. Then the Garden Director laughed. John was very relieved.

'What do I do? That's a very good question.'

There was another silence as the director looked at the Big House. He seemed to be struggling to find an answer.

'I have a lot of meetings. Meetings with bankers, with journalists, with agencies, with consultants. Then, of course, I have meetings with the board, with the Planning Director, the Financial Director, the Sales Director, the Personnel Director, the Operations Director and so on and so forth.'

John thought for a while. The director was also quiet, as if thinking about all those meetings.

'So your job is to have meetings.'

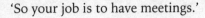

I have a lot of meetings. Meetings with bankers, with journalists, with agencies, with consultants and so on and so forth.

'It's more than that. I am ultimately in control of The Gardens. The buck stops with me.'

'So you have to decide the overall plan for the garden. For example, if there's going to be a Chinese Garden.'

'I have consultants to help me with that kind of thing. But, yes, overall I set the vision and overall strategy for the garden.'

John paused again. He already felt he was going too far, but the questions had a certain logic he wanted to follow.

'What is the vision for the garden?'

'It's laid out in our mission statement. You've got a copy in your hut.'

There was a pause while John visualized the mission statement, which was pinned facing the wall to allow the other side to display the lunch rota. There was another awkward silence, John made a move to go.

'Actually, that's not my mission statement. That was done by my predecessor. I've got different ideas.'

'Different ideas?'

'Yes, big plans. Really radical plans. They'll shake up the whole garden.'

'Shake up the garden?' John didn't know much about management but he did know that gardens didn't respond well to being shaken up.

'Yes, the bankers say we need something radical to get our visitor numbers up,' the director said.

John was getting more and more confused. What did bankers know about gardening. 'Have you talked to the gardeners about what they think?'

'Of course we have,' the director replied confidently. 'We've had the feedback from "Planting the seeds of growth".'

'And what was it?'

'I don't know yet. Our consultants are typing up the results and I'll get an executive summary. But I'm sure it will all be valuable input.'

John felt an irrational disappointment that his thought about the various gardens working together didn't seem to have had an effect on the director.

'Communication is absolutely vital to the business,' the director said forcefully. 'Since you ask, I'm actually getting in some top consultants to audit our communication across the whole garden. And if there's anything that's not working or needs improving, we'll put it right. What do you think about communication in the garden, John?'

'I think that there's . . .' John began.

> *If we want to succeed in the future, we've got to become a world-class, learning, knowledge-based organization.*

'Because communication is my number one priority,' the director continued. 'If we get that right then ideas can flow freely around the company. We can become a learning, knowledge-based organization.'

'A learning, knowledge-based organization?' John repeated.

'Yes, it's what our consultants say is industry best practice. And we've got to benchmark that. If we want to succeed in the future, we've got to become a world-class, learning, knowledge-based organization.'

'I thought we were a garden,' John said quietly.

The Garden Director shook his head as if to say that there was a lot John had to learn about the complexities of senior management.

The director suddenly looked at his watch. 'Well Brian, it's been good talking to you. I've got back-to-back meetings to go to now, but remember my door is always open.'

'Right,' said John, wondering who Brian was.

'There's another slat missing from this bench.' The director said as he got up. 'I thought I'd told someone to fix it. That's the trouble with this garden. Too much empowerment and not enough people using their initiative.'

ॐ When people make it to the top they start thinking that because they're at the top they must in some way be better than the people below them.

ॐ In truth they're probably better at the kind of things that get you promotion. Sadly, the skills needed to get to the top aren't always the ones needed when you're at the top.

ॐ In some organizations, the secret of rapid promotion is to take an initiative, take the credit and then move on before the consequences of the initiative become clear.

ॐ It doesn't look good on your CV that you've been responsible for slow and steady growth. Bold, high-profile initiatives look better. Especially if they include communication, learning and empowerment.

၆ That's why you should beware of managers who swap companies every two or three years. Often they've got to the top by moving fast enough to keep ahead of their mistakes. Once they're at the top they're in a position to make really big mistakes.

၆ People at the top forget that an organization, like nature, generally looks after itself. They think they can improve on nature. They wonder whether it would be a good idea to change things. Often they think change is expected of them.

၆ They can't ask anyone below them, so they ask somebody whose opinion they can respect. They ask consultants. And the consultants say that change would be a good thing. Because consultants don't get paid unless they can find something that needs changing.

Chapter Five

The Big Plan

As usual, John arrived early in the garden. It was a beautiful summer's day, the sky was clear and all was right with the world.

Then, as John approached the South gate, his eye was caught by a big new sign with the word 'Horticultura' painted on it in large, aggressive lettering. Underneath in smaller type it said: 'The new name for The Gardens'.

This came as a bit of a shock to John. No-one had told him that he now worked for Horticultura. He didn't particularly like the sound of it.

> Up the road to the Big House, as far as the eye could see, were parked bulldozers, diggers and earth-moving equipment.

John got a further shock when he passed through the gates. Up the road to the Big House, as far as the eye could see, were parked bulldozers, diggers and earth-moving equipment. John wondered what was going on but he was sure that it would all be explained in that morning's team meeting.

In the meeting, Kevin stood up and asked everyone to be quiet. It took some time before the room settled, because all the gardeners were discussing the new signs and the lines of diggers. Catherine, who came to work through the North gate, said there was a new sign and another line of diggers at that end of the garden too.

'I expect you're all wondering about the diggers,' Kevin started, 'and what Horticultura is all about.'

'It's Latin for bullshit,' a voice from the back said, to general laughter.

'I've got a briefing here that makes it all very clear.' There was a note of bitterness in Kevin's voice that caught everyone's attention and the room quietened.

'As part of the Planting the Seeds of Growth Programme,' Kevin read from his piece of paper, 'and as part of our continuous improvement to exceed customers' expectations and become a world-class garden . . .'

Kevin adjusted his glasses and the room held its breath.

'. . . we are radically restructuring the gardens so that the North Garden will become the South Garden and the East Garden will become the West Garden. This new, streamlined, customer-focused garden has been renamed Horticultura to reflect its new dynamism and passion for excellence.'

No-one in the room said anything. They knew from bitter experience that there was more to come.

'The investment required for this radical restructuring has been generated by the empowerment of a more responsive, flexible work-force.' Kevin took a breath '. . . and a programme of voluntary redundancies.'

There was a collective groan in the room.

'How much are they offering?' came the voice from the back.

'The redundancy package will be explained to you at the Big House when you apply.'

'Any other questions?' Kevin asked. But before anyone could reply, the room shook as a hundred bulldozers started their engines.

John was too shocked to do much work that morning. Instead he wandered up to his favourite part of the garden, a little clearing in a deciduous copse that was usually an oasis of calm filled with the heady fragrance of summer jasmine. He sat quietly on an old tree stump beneath a large oak and listened to the background roar of the bulldozers dispersing around the gardens.

Not long after, he was surprised to see the Garden Director enter the clearing with another man who was carrying a notepad. John sat quite still and they didn't seem to notice him. In fact they walked right past and sat down almost directly in front of him on a rickety old bench covered in grey-green lichen.

'Well that sounds like a pretty comprehensive plan,' the man with the notebook was saying. 'I think the analysts will be impressed.'

'Of course it's not the analysts we're interested in, it's our customers.'

'Of course,' replied the journalist, 'but the analysts will be impressed. They like to see pro-active management.'

'And of course our people. It's for them as well,' the director added.

'Of course. The analysts will like your people strategy.'

John wondered who the analysts were and why they needed to be impressed. He couldn't remember meeting any analysts in the garden.

'We consulted widely with our people,' the Garden Director said earnestly.

John tried to remember being consulted and then he remembered his sticky note.

'And we're providing counselling for those taking voluntary redundancy,' the director added.

'It sounds like you've given this a lot of thought.'

'Oh yes, we have the very best consultants.'

'Consultants.' The journalist nodded. 'The analysts will like that.'

After a while the two moved off and John was left alone. He walked thoughtfully back to the gardeners' hut for lunch, passing a crowd of visitors taking photos of each other in front of a glorious display of wisteria. The visitors were happy, the Garden Director was happy, the journalist was happy, the analysts were happy, so why did he feel so miserable?

John cheered up slightly when he saw his friend Steve outside the meeting room.

'John, I'm taking the money and running,' Steve told him, looking slightly shamefaced.

John winced. 'You can't do that, Steve, you know more about the garden than anyone.'

'There's not much point knowing stuff if you can't do stuff.' Steve patted him on the back. 'Don't look so miserable. Go and see a counsellor.'

'You can't do that,' said Kevin as he arrived for lunch. 'They've all taken voluntary redundancy.'

The next day the destruction would start and The Gardens would never be the same again.

That afternoon John walked back to his favourite spot to think about whether he too should take the money and run. Round every corner bulldozers or diggers sat, like a silent army waiting for battle. Their engines were off now and the only sounds John could hear were birds singing and visitors laughing. The next day the destruction would start and The Gardens would never be the same again.

John arrived at his old bench just in time to see a large lady being placed on a stretcher by two paramedics. She had fallen through the bottom of the bench where the rotten slats had finally given up and given way. As he helped remove the remains of the bench John shook his head.

Why couldn't the cost of the diesel in one of those bulldozers, the cost of repainting one sign, the cost of one consultant clearing his throat – why couldn't those pennies have been spent on fixing that one single bench so a woman could sit on it in peace and enjoy the jasmine without injuring herself?

John suddenly felt very angry and then equally suddenly felt very calm. The Garden Director had said that his door was always open. John decided that now was the time to see if it really was.

In a normal organization you would have thought that people at the bottom would look up and that people at the top would look down. In fact the reverse is often true.

People at the bottom sometimes never look up because they think their natural place is at the bottom.

At the other end of an organization, people who've made it to the top sometimes can't break their habit of looking upwards. They continually look up to bankers, shareholders, journalists and to other industry leaders.

❧ Even at the very top they still want approval. And when people need approval they start doing things to get attention.

❧ Analysts and journalists don't like small print. They like big stories. And that means big plans. The financial markets are driven by fear and greed. These are fed by big stories, which also mean big plans.

❧ All this explains why big bosses so often jump to big solutions without clearly identifying what the original problems were, if indeed there was one at all.

❧ Bosses reorganize, replan, restructure and re-engineer because they can, and because they feel they should. All three things are necessary occasionally but they are the exception rather than the rule.

❧ Occasionally the big plan is amazingly successful and becomes a case study in business schools. More often than not the plan fails and the organization only survives through more blood-letting and heavy-handed butchery thinly disguised as restructuring.

❧ Two groups of people leave during these upheavals – your best people and your best customers.

Chapter Six

After the Storm

John arrived late for work the following morning. The ground was sodden and there were large puddles on the paths. There had been a terrific storm the night before but now the sun was out and the garden was slowly drying.

By the time he got to the South Garden hut, word had spread of his attempt to storm the Big House the previous evening.

'Come to collect your things have you?' Steve said as soon as John entered the hut.

John tried to laugh but he knew there was every chance that this would be the last day he worked in the garden.

The other gardeners gathered round John.

'Did you tell him what he could do with his garden, John?' a voice from the back said.

'Did you actually get to speak to him?' Catherine asked, slightly more sympathetically.

Clearly, the hut was expecting John to tell them all about his meeting with the Garden Director. Someone passed him a cup of coffee, so he drew up a battered chair and got ready to tell his story.

'When I got there,' John started, 'he was in a meeting. I told his secretary about his door always being open and she said that it would next be open on a Tuesday afternoon next month for half an hour.'

'What did you do?' Catherine asked.

'I waited for three hours and fifteen minutes.' John sipped his coffee. 'When he finally came out I told him that his door was now open and I'd like to speak to him.'

'Did he sack you then or will he be doing it today?' the voice from the back said.

'He thought about it and then invited me in.'

'What's his office like?' Steve asked.

'It's about as big as this hut. It was full of all the plans for the new gardens and Horticultura and all that stuff. He saw me looking at them and then started taking me through them all. He started all enthusiastically but when I didn't say anything he slowly ran out of steam.'

'Good luck in your new job, pal,' the voice from the back chipped in encouragingly.

'Shut up, Louis,' Kevin told him bluntly. 'What happened then?'

'There was a long silence and then I told him that he was making a big mistake.'

There was a collective intake of breath around the room. Heads were shaken, mental goodbye notes were written.

The conversation had lasted until ten to one in the morning and when it was over, John was so mentally and emotionally drained he could barely find his way home.

John remembered the conversation that he'd then had with the director, who had started calm, then become very angry and finally was calm again. The conversation had lasted until ten to one in the morning and when it was over, John was so mentally and emotionally drained he could barely find his way home.

'I told him that his thinking was completely upside down, back to front and inside out. I told him we had a good garden with good people working in it. I told him that if he helped us we could make it a really great garden.'

'And then he told you that we were already empowered,' Steve guessed.

'Er, yes,' John conceded. 'In fact he got quite angry and said that we'd been empowered seven times at great expense by top consultants and if we weren't empowered now we never would be. I then told him that every time we were empowered, people lost their jobs and the people most likely to leave were those with the most initiative.'

'Spot on,' said Steve, nodding his head.

'In fact I probably overdid it and told him that voluntary redundancy programmes generally amounted to dead wood retention programmes.'

Kevin smiled and shook his head.

John carried on, suddenly feeling he didn't have much time left. 'I then told him that his plans for restructuring the garden were likely to be disastrous. He got very angry again, pointed to the plans and said that some of the best brains in the country had worked on those plans. He kept mentioning MBAs, whatever they are. I waited until he'd stopped shouting and then I told him they would all be a disaster.'

'You're either very brave or very stupid, John,' Kevin said in a hushed, amazed tone.

'He then went very calm and quiet, sat behind his desk and said, "OK, John, what would you do?"'

'Yes, what would you do, John,' Steve asked.

John paused, suddenly feeling slightly embarrassed.

'Go on, John,' Kevin prompted. 'Tell us what you told him.'

'I told him that he should stop empowering us and start trusting us.' John took a deep breath and continued, 'I told him that instead of talking to us he should listen to us. I told him that instead of pruning and replanting he should try watering and feeding. I told him that bankers, analysts and journalists couldn't grow a radish between them. I told him that he should sack his consultants and get his managers to do what they're paid for. I told him all the managers should come out of the Big House and see what their decisions actually mean in the garden. And then, finally, I pointed to all his big colour plans in the room, and told him that if he'd give us the tools we could do the job ourselves.'

The colossal machine shuddered past him and then veered directly on to the beautifully manicured lawns.

There was a spontaneous round of applause in the room. When it had died out, Kevin asked the question that was in everybody's mind.

'And then what did he say?'

'Nothing. He asked me to repeat everything.'

'He was probably taping it for your tribunal,' cheery Louis said from the back.

John remembered that he had had to repeat everything he'd said several times. Each time he'd filled in more and more detail. He didn't know where it came from, it just seemed to have a natural logic. Finally, at nearly one o'clock, the Garden

Director stood up and said: 'Thanks for coming in. We'll talk more about this later.'

It was then obvious to John that the interview was over and that the door was now closed. He'd walked back home in the pouring rain, feeling wetter and more miserable with every step.

John spent a few more minutes answering questions from the gardeners, before he stood up and said, 'Well, I'm off to enjoy my last day at work.'

As there was a very good chance that it would be his last day in the job, John chose to work up by the East Garden in amongst the big oaks that had been there long before the gardens, the Big House and everyone else. It was a lovely sunny morning with a cool breeze and John worked away contentedly, almost forgetting the night before, until he suddenly heard the noise of a huge bulldozer engine starting up nearby.

John stood bolt upright and saw the big yellow beast shuddering as the driver revved its diesel engine. After a few seconds, it jolted forward. John stood frozen to the spot, unable to think or speak.

The colossal machine shuddered past him and then veered directly on to the beautifully manicured lawns. It turned in a perfect wide half circle on the lawn and then lumbered back on to the road and out away towards the exit.

And then, one by one, the bulldozers emerged from their resting places all over the garden, clanked past him and disappeared down and out of the South gates.

John looked at the deep track marks gouged into the almost perfect lawn and laughed. Then, as the cool breeze dispersed the diesel fumes, he went back to work.

ᴧ Company cultures are stubborn things. You can't change them overnight. But they can be changed. Company cultures can grow up in the same way humans can grow up. How it grows depends on its role models, its education and its environment.

ᴧ The role of the big boss is therefore critical.

ᴧ The big boss only has two vital functions: to decide on the vision and strategy for the organization and then to make sure the entire organization delivers that vision.

ᴧ The big boss therefore must have two core skills: the ability to have a strategic vision and the ability to communicate the vision to those who make it happen. In short, they need to *direct* and they need to *manage*. That's why they're called managing directors.

ᴧ If you want a grown-up company, you need a grown-up managing director in charge of grown-up managers.

☙ This requires managers to do less command and control and more boundary setting and facilitation.

☙ Ironically, only a very strong, very confident, very disciplined manager can do this.

☙ For many managers, it means a big personal change, which is a lot harder than having a big plan.

Chapter Seven

Sweeping Up

When John arrived for work the following day he could smell wood smoke. This was quite unusual in the garden as any kind of burning needed special permission from the Director of Planning. On his way up through the South Garden he came across the smouldering remains of a large number of Horticultura signs. John smiled and he was filled with hope that, for once, things in the garden might be taking a turn for the better.

Kevin was also in a good mood that morning in the team meeting.

'Good morning, everyone,' he said to the assembled gardeners, 'there's good news and bad news.'

This announcement brought the meeting to attention. Given the recent events, they wouldn't have been surprised at any news, good or bad.

'The good news is that the consultants have gone, Horticultura is dead and buried and there isn't going to be any voluntary redundancy.' There was a loud cheer among the gardeners.

The bad news ...' Kevin continued, '. . . is compulsory redundancies,' a voice from the back said to more laughter.

'If there are, Louis,' Kevin replied, 'you'll be the first to go.' There was another loud cheer among the gardeners.

'The bad news is that we've got to clear up the mess. I need a working party to start repairing the lawns after our bull-dozer friends practised their handbrake turns on them.'

A couple of hands went up, John amongst them.

'OK everybody, let's get back to work.'

'What, is that it?' Louis asked from the back. 'No initiatives, no empowerment. No brave new world.'

'No, that's it.'

'I'm not happy.' Louis insisted. 'I demand to be radically restructured. Or re-vectored. Or re-engineered. I don't mind which.'

> *I need a working party to start repairing the lawns after our bulldozer friends practised their handbrake turns on them.*

'Let's just get back to work, everybody. We've got plenty of it.'

A week passed where nothing happened in the gardens apart from work carrying on, more or less as normal. But at the next team meeting, something odd and rather refreshing happened. There was a message from the Big House thanking everyone for their help in repairing the lawns. There was also a request from the Head of Planning for another working party.

'I need a couple of people to repair the benches around the gardens,' Kevin said. 'Priority from Planning.'

Catherine put her hand up. 'I wouldn't mind doing that. I like working with wood.'

'Thank you Catherine. You can start in the North Garden. Apparently they've got the most damaged benches.'

'The North Garden?' Catherine said, clearly quite shocked. The North Garden was somewhere you went only if you were on your way home or had a friend who worked there.

Kevin checked his piece of paper. 'That's what it says. Oh and they'll be a couple of people from the East Garden planting some spare begonias over here.'

John remembered his original sticky note from the 'Planting the seeds of growth' session and he wondered.

Over the next few weeks, more age-old problems were tackled. The gardens themselves didn't change much but many of the little minor irritations for visitor and gardener alike were put right. Naturally, it all cost money but someone, somewhere, had decided that money needed to be spent.

John himself had installed a child safety rail on a bridge in the ornamental gardens. Again this was something that everyone knew needed doing but had never quite been a priority. Now it was fixed and John felt good about it. Then, towards the beginning of autumn when the leaves were just beginning to turn gold and brown, there was a remarkable team meeting where two things happened. Looking back on it, John was very pleased that the two things had happened together.

Kevin was standing in front of the group as usual, reading out the list of tasks to be done that week. A few of the tasks were problems that had needed fixing for a long time but most of them were now new ideas for improvements. These were things that had been noticed by the gardeners and that they wanted time and permission to put right. They were suggested to Kevin, he checked with the Big House and, nine times out of ten, they were on the task list the following week.

A few of the tasks were problems that had needed fixing for a long time but most of them were now new ideas for improvements.

'Due to your hard work over the past few weeks,' Kevin was saying, 'and because you are people and therefore our greatest asset, the management have decided to refurbish our hut.'

There were loud cheers around the room and several immediate and impractical suggestions concerning the purchase and installation of pool tables, Jacuzzis and free bars.

At that moment, while everyone was enjoying themselves, the Garden Director slipped unnoticed into the back of the meeting and sat down quietly.

'This is obviously a good management decision,' Kevin continued, enjoying his role as the bringer of good news. 'They've also decided to ask for our input on what the new meeting room should be like, which is a very brave management decision.'

Kevin spotted the director sitting at the back but, before he could say anything, the director put his finger to his lips and motioned for Kevin to continue.

'So we need to hear some sensible ideas from you,' Kevin said to the group.

'I've got an idea.' It was Louis. John winced. It was unlikely to be a good idea. In fact it was likely to be a fantastically rude idea.

'Instead of having four small huts in the separate gardens, why don't we have one big hut. We'd all get better facilities and it would probably be cheaper than four small huts.'

The room was stunned. Not because the idea was good, which it clearly was, but that it had come from Louis, the world's biggest cynic.

John turned to see what the director thought and was just in time to see him slip quietly from the room.

Shortly afterwards, a working party was appointed to help design the new gardeners' meeting hut. There was to be one big hut for all four gardens. One gardener was appointed from each of the gardens to help design the hut. Louis volunteered to be the representative from the South Garden.

ॐ Getting people to take initiative requires two essential elements: they need permission and they need trust.

ॐ Even when people are given permission to take the initiative, be creative and generally take responsibility for their actions, they won't do any of these things unless there is also a basis of trust.

ॐ People must trust that when they have an idea or take an initiative, their actions will be welcomed, encouraged and supported by management.

ॐ That trust needs to be earned.

ॐ Trust isn't built by mission statements, consultants or big speeches. Trust is earned by the continual repetition of the right things done at the right time in the right way. A pattern of trust is established when people understand and accept it without thinking.

ॐ Sometimes when there is a history of mistrust, there needs to be clear signal that things have changed. But this signal must be a concrete management action. In business, as in politics, people have seen too many signals and not enough trains.

❧ Investing money in the ideas and concerns of people is the clearest possible sign.

❧ Trying to put everything right at once generally creates more problems than it solves. But putting a few small things right has a very big impact.

❧ Having straightened out the things that frustrate people, you can then concentrate on the things that inspire and engage people.

Chapter Eight

Landscaping

Winter had arrived in the garden and there was a general feeling that the year had ended well. There had been no radical changes of layout or organization but things seemed to be working better. Most gardeners had decided to stay on after the events of the summer and the teams were now settled. Team meetings ran smoothly with problems being aired freely and tackled promptly. There had even been a small increase in visitor numbers.

One of the many events that had passed almost unnoticed was the launch by the Garden Director of the new mission statement and vision and values for the garden. He'd popped into one of the team meetings, which wasn't in itself unusual anymore, and asked if he could talk to the team about the future direction of the gardens.

The Garden Director told everyone that he'd thought a great deal about The Gardens over the previous months and that now he had a clear vision of what the garden should be. He said he wanted The Gardens to be a leading example of an informal landscaped garden with special emphasis on native trees, shrubs and flowers, much like the classic English gardens of the 18th century. The Garden Director then asked the gardeners for their thoughts.

'So this means we're not going to become a theme park with rides and that sort of thing,' Louis clarified.

'Definitely not,' the director replied. 'Nothing wrong with that but that's not the way we're going to go.'

'What about the other way. Are we going to become a garden centre and nursery,' Catherine asked.

'No, we're not going to do that either. We're going to be a garden for people who love gardens.'

There were nods of agreement around the room. That was the kind of future they could believe in. They were gardeners after all.

> There were nods of agreement around the room. That was the kind of future they could believe in. They were gardeners after all.

'Now what about our vision and values?' the director asked to a silent audience. The gardeners had heard 'vision and values' a million times before.

The director smiled. 'I'll let you guess. What do you think they are?'

'Delighting the customer by exceeding their expectations?' Louis suggested helpfully.

'Benchmarking best practice,' someone shouted from the back.

Then the flood gates opened and the room was filled with shouts of assets, transparency, environment, focus, value, community, empowerment, trust, loyalty and some words that weren't printable in any statement.

'Thank you very much, everyone. I see the years of internal communication haven't been wasted.' The director waited for the laughter to subside. When the room was silent again, he continued, 'We know what kind of garden we want to be now. The way we're going to get there is by being the best possible place to visit and the best possible place to work. And that's it.'

No-one said anything. It seemed such good sense that there wasn't anything to say.

'And if anything we do doesn't contribute to making us the best possible place to visit or the best possible place to work, then we don't do it. Full stop.'

Six months ago they wouldn't have believed a word he said. Six months ago they probably wouldn't have listened to a word he said. But now they knew that things happened in the garden and they generally happened for the right reasons.

John thought of that meeting as he walked through the crisp morning air towards the new meeting hut. There wasn't a person in the garden who didn't know what kind of garden they were building and how they were going to do it.

John arrived at the meeting room glad to step into the warmth and out of the winter chill. Many of the other gardeners were already there, eating their cooked breakfasts. It was one of the many innovations suggested by Louis and his working party at the planning stage.

'Morning John.' As John joined the small queue for breakfast he was joined by a gardener called Jenny who had worked in the East Garden for more than twenty years. John had met her in a working party to discuss surgery for the big trees dotted all round the gardens.

Without any formal restructuring, the divisions of the garden into North, South, East and West had become no more than place names.

'We're going to have a look at those Poplars today,' Jenny said.

There were a couple of poplars in the West Garden that weren't very well. Jenny had quickly shown that it was a drainage problem, something that John would never have guessed from a million years staring at the tree.

One of the side-effects of Louis' initial idea for one canteen had been the discovery that there was a vast amount of expertise in the organization. Jenny knew a lot about trees and actually had a doctorate to her name, although she always kept quiet about it.

Task forces of gardeners working across the gardens were now the rule rather than the exception. So much so that, without any formal restructuring, the divisions of the garden into North, South, East and West had become no more than place names.

Of course, none of these changes would have been able to happen were it not for a subtle but deep-rooted change in the Big House.

✿ Healthy, organic growth comes from a few business fundamentals. One of them is that the whole organization knows what it is doing and feels able to do it.

✿ Sadly, mission statements are generally a collection of clichés that have had the meaning beaten out of them long ago.

✿ People need two things in life to be happy: they need to have some sort of meaningful purpose and they need to have rules for what they can and can't do.

✿ Organizations are no different. Goals should be very ambitious so that they are a real challenge but also very simple to understand.

ॐ Naturally, goals will change over time but they should always be clear enough and far enough away to make the direction of everyone's efforts obvious.

ॐ Values have become even more hollow and meaningless than mission statements.

ॐ Real values are those that you are prepared to enforce. In other words they are the rules. Break them and you're out. That's how cultures are forged and maintained.

ॐ When the purpose is clear and the rules are straight, the effort and initiatives of everyone will naturally align. Processes, structures and habits inconsistent with this purpose that break the rules will either be actively discarded or passively ignored.

ॐ Department or team structures that make no sense will go, along with the silo or smokestack mentality that they often breed.

Chapter Nine

Seeds for Growth

John grabbed himself a bacon sandwich and joined Catherine who was at the far end of the room in front of a large map of The Gardens. Catherine was talking to Adam, the Head of Planning, who often popped in at breakfast to talk through plans and get the input of the gardeners. In fact, over the past few months it had become noticeable that Adam spent more time with the gardeners than he did at the Big House.

The Big House was where the central planning happened. It was where the big decisions were made about what was to be planted and what was to be cleared. It was also where a host of smaller decisions were made about when watering, seeding, composting and mowing were to be done. Most of all, the Big House planned the use of people. They planned in detail who should do what by when and how many people were needed to do it.

The people in the Big House were well educated and good with figures. For many years the Garden Director relied on them completely. After all, every time he asked for a cost saving, they had delivered it. So effective had they become in weeding out costs, that the people in the Big House were able to destroy costs as soon as they raised their ugly little heads – even before they knew whether it was a weed or an important new plant.

Until John had walked through the Garden Director's open door, the Big House had insulated the Garden Director from ever having to talk to the gardeners. And because the Big House were clearly delivering what the Garden Director wanted, they never bothered speaking to the gardeners either. But that had now changed and Adam was living proof of it.

Rumour had it that Adam had gone on one of the communication courses the supervisors were put through regularly. It had come as quite a wake up call for him that communication was seen as the weakest skill for him personally and for the board in general. To his credit he had now remedied the situation and was a full-time practitioner of good communication, especially now that his divorce was out of the way.

> *Until John had walked through the Garden Director's open door, the Big House had insulated the Garden Director from ever having to talk to the gardeners.*

'Putting this map up was one of the best ideas of the working party,' Adam was saying.

'That's because we can actually see the big picture now,' Catherine said. 'We now get some idea of the thinking behind all your plans.'

'That's the frightening bit,' Adam said with a laugh.

'Well, now we know what we're doing, we can help you plan it.'

'That's right. I might as well take early retirement.'

Adam could afford to joke about early retirement. Two directors from the Big House had already taken early retirement at around the same time the bulldozers left the garden. Their departure had had a similar uplifting effect throughout the garden.

Word had it that these directors thought they didn't need training.

'Adam, come and have a look at the board,' John said, motioning them to join him on the other side of the room where there was a huge whiteboard. The whiteboard was headed: 'A better place to visit and work.' Across it, people had written in marker pens various ideas for achieving one or both aims. Some of the ideas had been circled and initialled by the person who was making the idea happen.

'What's new this week, John?' Adam asked, as he scanned the board.

'It's pretty much all stuff we can sort out down here, but here's one for you.' John pointed to a note on the board. 'Order seeds later to reduce wastage,' he read.

'What's the thought behind that one?' Adam asked.

'Well, you know we order seeds five years in advance and in bulk to reduce cost.'

'Yes.' Adam braced himself. He'd learned a lot since he'd started working with the gardeners and most of it didn't reflect well on the Big House.

'By the time we actually need it, about half of it has rotted or been eaten by rats. So, in fact, we're buying twice as much seed as we need. Wasting half the money.'

'Point taken,' Adam nodded.

'What we need is to be able to order the seeds when we need them,' Catherine added.

'Yes but . . .' Adam started nervously, with visions of garden-ers ordering seeds one packet at a time.

'We just need a more flexible, long-term contract with the seed suppliers,' Catherine insisted.

'OK. I'll get my contracts guy to have a look at it. Who's going to work with him to cover the seed angle?'

Catherine took a marker pen and circled the idea on the board.

'Better put my initials on it because I wrote it.'

Afterwards John spent a pleasant morning working with Steve in different areas of the garden. He probably worked harder than when he started but because the work was more varied and it all seemed to have a purpose, he didn't mind. On his way back to the hut for lunch, they spotted Kevin the team leader putting up a bird box on a tree. John did a slight double-take.

> *He probably worked harder than when he started but because the work was more varied and it all seemed to have a purpose, he didn't mind.*

'Isn't that our old suggestion box?' Steve asked as Kevin finished hammering a nail in.

'Yep. Best place for it. At its most productive it produced an old chocolate wrapper and a bus ticket.'

John stared up at it. He could just about make out the old 'Digging for the Future' logo on it from a long-forgotten empowerment.

'What's new in the garden, then?' Kevin asked them as they all walked back to the hut.

'We've got a suggestion box up a tree,' Steve said helpfully.

'That's not quite what I meant,' Kevin laughed. 'Do you know something? Since I went away on my course, I'm now measured on what we've contributed to better working and visiting.'

'It's in your job spec?' John raised his eyebrows in surprise.

'Yes. And it'll be in yours shortly,' Kevin replied.

'Do they pay us for all these ideas?' John asked.

'Put it this way, they'll pay for the ideas to happen and they won't pay you if the ideas don't happen,' Kevin explained.

'I suppose that's better than paying for you not to have ideas and then not paying for ideas that you do have,' Steve said.

'Do you think it'll work?' John asked mischievously.

'Well Steve's still here,' Kevin said, thumping Steve on the shoulder, 'so it can't be all bad.'

A week later at the team meeting Kevin made a small announcement.

'As from next month the gardeners have full budgetary responsibility for buying seed.'

'Let's go shopping!' Louis shouted from the back.

'We're going to be sorting out what we need and the best way to get it,' Catherine said. 'If we do it right, which we will, we'll be able to get some of the other stuff we wanted.'

It turned out that seed buying was only the start. Over the weeks and months that followed, responsibility for all sorts of budgets found its way down to the people who could actually see how it was spent.

And, strangest of all, they knew exactly how to look after the money, just as they did at home.

❧ Sometimes it's hard to remember that the aim of empowering people is to release their potential to grow the business.

❧ There's an old saying the Greek philosophers were fond of: money talks, bullshit walks.

❧ If you really trust your people, if you really want them to take the initiative, if you really want them to take responsibility for growing their part of the business, then you need to trust them with something important.

❧ Money.

❧ You can tell a lot about an organization by how far up or down the level of budget responsibility sits.

❧ If the purchase of an additional paperclip needs the approval of the managing director, you're in trouble. Why? Because your managing director is spending too much time signing off expenditure and not doing his two vital tasks, managing and directing.

❧ The lower down the organization budgetary responsibility lies, the more responsible the organization will be. People will know what things cost and where the money comes from. They will also be in the best position to decide where money is most effectively spent or not spent.

୶ When people also know they'll be paid more for improving the business and managing their budgets better, you'll have the best of all possible worlds.

୶ And what happens to managers when their teams are looking after themselves? They get to spend less time controlling and more time taking the initiative and thinking creatively for themselves.

୶ So you have managers who are free to think, free to act and free to deliver profit.

Chapter Ten

Grass Roots

High above the gardens, the tall lime trees swayed gently in the early summer breeze. It was almost a year since John had started work in the gardens and now he was waiting at the South gate to greet a new gardener who was starting that day. Outside the gate there was already a steady line of people queuing at the turnstile to get in the garden and coaches were manoeuvring in the car park prior to disgorging their loads of day trippers from far and wide.

John noticed a garden guide in a smart green uniform welcoming the parties of visitors, explaining what was what and sending them on their way with a smile. It was the security guard who had welcomed him on his first day.

'Hello there, are you John?' a voice said behind him.

John turned and saw a man roughly the same age as him. 'That's me,' he said shaking the man's hand. 'Welcome to the Gardens. Come with me and I'll show you around.'

The new gardener's name was Leon. John walked with him up through the South Garden towards the Big House.

'This garden's in pretty good shape,' Leon remarked, casting a professional eye over the shrubberies and beds.

'We do our best,' John said proudly, realizing just how far they'd come in a year. 'You've come from the Kingsmoor Garden haven't you?'

'Florex, please,' Leon replied. 'That's what they're called now.'

'Voluntary redundancy?'

'That's right. Best thing that ever happened in Kingsmoor, sorry Florex. Couldn't wait to get out.'

'Things are different here,' John reassured him.

'So I've heard,' Leon said, looking around him approvingly.

The two gardeners turned right into a little lane that ran past some workshops. Inside was a group of gardeners looking intently at the engine of a small tractor.

'Problems with your tractors?' Leon asked. 'Ours were blowing up the whole time.'

'That's actually a training course,' John explained as he waved to the group. 'We did have a lot of problems with the tractors and they were out of action for days while we waited for the engineers.'

'Or weeks,' Leon added.

'Exactly. We decided we didn't want to wait that long. In an ideal world we would fix them ourselves. So we talked it through with the Big House and they organized the training for us. Now we get trained on the basics and we can fix most breakdowns ourselves.'

'Sounds like more work to me.' Leon looked doubtful.

'It's actually less work. It's a lot harder to work without a tractor. Plus the more you fix round here the more you get paid.'

'Really?' Leon's eyebrows shot up.

'Oh yes,' John said. 'You're paid to improve the way we work or the visitor experience. Even if that just means being a good gardener, good with the visitors or a good team member.'

'That sounds good.'

> *And everything everyone does in the garden from top to bottom is to make working here more enjoyable and visiting The Gardens more enjoyable.*

'By the way, I think I've just given you your induction.'

'I'm sorry?' Leon looked confused.

'The aim of the garden is to be the best possible traditional landscaped garden.'

'OK,' Leon nodded.

'And everything everyone does in the garden from top to bottom is to make working here more enjoyable and visiting The Gardens more enjoyable.'

'And that's it?' Leon said, surprised.

'Yes. It sounds simple but it means you're always thinking about the whole garden rather than the bed you're digging.'

Over lunch, John introduced Leon to the rest of the gardeners and they talked about the trouble in Leon's old gardens and how they'd overcome the same problems in The Gardens. The door suddenly burst open and Steve strode in.

'I've had a brilliant idea!' he announced to the whole room. 'We've been struggling with what to do with those old tropical gardens, well I've cracked it.'

'Well what is it?' Catherine asked.

Steve sat down next to John who squeezed in a quick introduction to Leon.

'Pleased to meet you Leon. You'll like it here,' Steve said without pausing for breath. 'I was talking to a family out in the West Garden and they said what they'd really like is a maze.'

'A maze, that's a brilliant idea,' John said. 'Why didn't anyone think of that before?'

'We did,' said Kevin who had joined them to hear the brilliant idea, 'but that was in the old days.'

'Well, let's do it this time,' Steve said enthusiastically. 'It's spot on for a traditional garden and the visitors will love it. In fact it's such a good idea that I'm going to have a chat with Adam now.'

And with that, Steve disappeared back out through the door. Throughout, Leon had sat wide-eyed and open-mouthed.

That afternoon, formalities and paper signing complete, John took Leon from the Big House back into the South Garden where they were due to re-lay some paths. They worked most of the afternoon with several other gardeners until the job had been completed. Then they gathered up their tools and walked back towards the gardeners' hut. Passing the tropical gardens, they found Steve and Adam, the Head of Planning, deep in conversation.

'Have you got your bonus yet?' John shouted to Steve.

'It's such a good idea, I'm beginning to thing I had it myself,' Adam replied.

As the gardeners gathered round him, Steve unrolled a pre-liminary sketch he'd done of how the maze would fit in the garden.

John suddenly had an idea. 'Why don't we have a competition to design the maze. Open to the public. Be great for publicity.'

The gardeners all started chipping in with ideas for how the maze could work and were so engaged they failed to notice the Garden Director arriving.

'You must be Leon, our new recruit,' the Garden Director said to Leon. 'I'm Martin.'

'Hello, Martin, pleased to meet you,' Leon replied as they shook hands.

The Garden Director moved across to the group discussion. 'So Steve, this is the maze idea. I've heard all about it.'

'Well, good news travels fast,' Steve said with a grin.

'It's a great idea. What do you think, Adam?'

'It's a winner,' Adam declared, nodding his head. 'The competition is also a good idea. I say let's go with it.'

The Garden Director smiled. 'You know John and Steve, you should be running the garden.'

John and Steve looked at the Garden Director and also smiled.

'We do run the garden,' John said.

The gardeners all started chipping in with ideas for how the maze could work and were so engaged they failed to notice the Garden Director arriving.

A company with a healthy and productive culture is one where top-down inspiration meets bottom-up energy.

People in this culture find greater individual productivity, greater job satisfaction and greater pride in the company. At the same time managers are freed up to think about the business and how to improve it.

If you want to start the change you need to start with communication.

Communication is what human beings use to inform, to instruct and, crucially, to motivate. And communication is successful only when it changes the way people think, feel and act.

First, decide what you want your company to think, feel and do. Once you've decided the purpose of your business, managers must then communicate this in everything they think, feel and do.

Little things will count as much as the big things. The way a team meeting is run is as important as the way a conference is run. The life of a small idea is as important as the life of a big idea. The way a single member of staff is managed is as important as the way the company is managed.

No organization is greater than the sum of its parts. And when you think of the huge consequences that come from the smallest of events, you'll know that in reality there are no small events.

ᥬ What you want at the top on the largest scale you have to have at the bottom on the smallest scale.

ᥬ If you want initiative and responsibility throughout the organization, you know where to start.

ᥬ At the grass roots.

Grass
Seeds

How to lead from the front and earn trust

1. Have a simple, clear vision

2. Passionately believe in your vision

3. Build a team that shares your vision

4. Work harder than anybody else

5. Understand the front line

6. Tell your team exactly what you expect of them

7. Listen to your team and respect their skills

8. Keep everyone informed and motivated

9. Give clear orders and make sure they happen

10. Share the profits

How to communicate so things change

---

1. Communication works when something changes

2. Tell it like it is – spin achieves nothing

3. Actions speak louder than words

4. Consistency is the clearest message

5. Listen before you think before you speak

6. If it really matters, do it face-to-face

7. Encourage feedback and act on it

8. Involvement is the best persuader

9. Think twice before e-mailing

10. Little and often is better than long and loud

How to change people's behaviour

1. Start with some praise for the person

2. Mention your own mistakes in the area

3. Understand the reasons for their old behaviour

4. Talk about the effects of their old behaviour

5. Explain the benefits of new behaviour

6. Make the first part of change the easiest

7. Make sure the changes mean no loss of face

8. Agree targets for changed behaviour

9. Make the changes worth their while

10. Monitor and encourage new behaviour

How to work smarter, not harder

1. Be clear about your agenda and stick to it

2. Get organized before you get an organizer

3. Start work half an hour earlier

4. Work in small digestible chunks

5. Think in the morning, do after lunch

6. Put thinking time in your diary

7. If you're not adding value, delegate

8. Only travel if you'll return richer or wiser

9. Keep your desk and in-box clear

10. Plan for tomorrow but act today

How to be a good people manager

1. Know what you need to achieve yourself

2. Establish mutual expectations from the start

3. Review working relationships while they still work

4. Don't take people for granted – thank them now

5. Manage in context – understand all sides

6. Discover the facts through pro-active listening

7. Acknowledge people's feelings – they affect work

8. Ask for solutions from those with problems

9. Go for lunch – you can't bond with a sandwich

10. Stay calm and keep a sense of humour – it's only work

How to innovate

1. Apply your area of expertise to your area of ignorance

2. Combine two good ideas into one better idea

3. Design it to look, feel and work better

4. Import or export an existing idea into a new market

5. Make it disposable or longer-lasting

6. Make it more exclusive or more accessible

7. Cut out the middleman and do it direct

8. Get in the middle and add value

9. Make a small thing bigger or a big thing smaller

10. Do it so it's quicker, easier or friendlier

How to create an innovation culture

---

1. Don't outsource your imagination to agencies

2. Make meetings more productive

3. Increase cross-functional contact

4. Allocate time and money for innovation

5. Have innovation as a measurable target

6. Hire interesting people

7. Have a canteen worth going to

8. Speed up and simplify decision making

9. Use research to identify needs

10. Make it a core part of everyone's job

How to satisfy existing customers and attract new ones

1. Don't keep them waiting – time is money

2. Get their details right – their name matters to them

3. Let them choose their channel

4. Act on their feedback before they act on it

5. Deliver what and when you promise

6. Keep them informed of both good news and bad

7. Make paperwork clear, easy and friendly

8. Involve customers in product development

9. Never compromise on quality

10. Invest in service if you want a long-term future

How to build a brand

1. Clearly define every aspect of the brand

2. Build both functional and emotional benefits

3. Communicate brand definition to all

4. Brand every detail of delivery

5. Be consistent in brand communication

6. Don't let outside agencies own your brand

7. Jealously guard brand equities

8. Train the people who deliver the brand

9. Constantly nurture affection for brand

10. Develop the brand through evolution, not revolution

How to manage a project successfully

1. Plan in detail

2. Build in flexibility with time and budget contingency

3. Have clearly defined objectives

4. Have clearly defined ownership of objectives

5. Check all assumptions are shared

6. Delegate specific tasks

7. Hold regular status meetings

8. Communicate problems early

9. Maintain full and clear records

10. Keep customers updated regularly

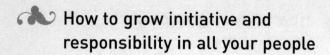 # How to grow initiative and responsibility in all your people

1. Have strong leaders prepared to change the culture

2. Build a management team who share the vision

3. Make sure your top people are top communicators

4. Downsize your consultants

5. Train your people in the skills core to your business

6. Build trust with your people by listening to them

7. Start the change by fixing things that don't work

8. Give your supervisors as much power as they can handle

9. Give people the budget to go with responsibility

10. Make improvement a core part of everyone's job

Enjoyed this book?

We hope so. And we'd love to hear from you – what you thought of it, your experiences of the areas covered in this book and how you think *Grass Roots Management* could make a difference to you and your business.

You can e-mail your comments direct to the author on **guy.browning@smokehouse.co.uk** and/or the publishers, Prentice Hall Business via our website **www.business-minds.com** (click on the feedback button).

So, whether you've got a real-life anecdote you'd like to share, or whether you want to tell us what you think and what you'd like to read more about, just drop us a line. We'd be delighted to hear from you.

Thanks

Guy Browning and Prentice Hall Business